Table of Contents

INTRODUCTION

Have you ever felt overwhelmed? We have many feelings. We have many thoughts. Sometimes, we need time to be quiet.

Meditation is a way for us to be still. It means to think deeply. It's the focusing of the mind for a period of time. Meditation is a way to relax. It leads us to a calm state of mind. It lets us see thoughts more clearly.

This book gives you tips on how to be **mindful**. Mindful means being aware. It means taking care of your body and mind. Take a moment. Practice being still. Just breathe …

Tip: Choose to be still.

Chapter One
Breathe with Purpose

Mindful breathing is a great way to still your mind and body. Breathe in. Breathe out. Take charge of your breathing. Controlled breathing is important for meditation. It calms nerves. It eases stress.

Breathe by making full use of the air by practicing this:

- Sit straight in a chair.
- Put your feet flat on floor. Put your hands in your lap.
- Close your eyes and mouth.
- Breathe in through your nose. Fill your lungs with air.
- Count to 4. Hold your breath for 4 seconds.
- Open your mouth. Slowly breathe out. Count to 4. Hold your breath for 4 seconds.
- Repeat this several times.

Tip: Take long, slow breaths when you feel anxious.

Practice breathing with your belly:

- Put your hands on your belly.
- Slowly breathe in and out through your nose.
- Feel your hands move with each breath.

Breathe like a humming bee:

- Close your mouth, but keep your teeth apart.
- Put 1 finger in each ear.
- Breathe in slowly through your nose. Breathe out slowly through your mouth.
- Make a long humming sound. Feel the **vibrations** of the hum in your head and chest. Vibrations are sound waves.

Practice these techniques for 5 minutes each. Start breathing normally. Be aware of your natural flow of breath. How do you feel?

Tip: Practice **yoga**. Do poses and mindful breathing at the same time.

CHAPTER TWO
Try Guided Meditation

Guided meditation is led by a leader. The leader gives step-by-step directions. There are different ways to practice guided meditation. Participants can listen to a tape. They can watch a video. They can go to a class.

Try "The Balloon":

- Sit or stand. Pretend your belly is a balloon.
- Breathe in. Fill your belly with air. Make your belly as big as you can. Stretch out your arms.
- Hold your breath for 4 seconds.
- Slowly breathe out the air through your nose. Make a hissing sound like a balloon. Feel your body relax.

Tip: Pretend you're being pulled from the top of your body. Stretch your body.

Try "Outer Space":

- Lie down.
- Close your eyes.
- Imagine your body becoming very light. Pretend your body has no weight. Pretend to float upward.
- Picture your body floating in outer space. Imagine your body floating in the dark. See your body floating among the stars.
- Enjoy how light and free your body is. Enjoy how light and free your mind is.
- Start floating back to Earth. Do this slowly.
- Start floating back to the room you're in.
- Feel your body becoming heavy again.
- Slowly move your toes.
- Slowly move your fingers.
- Breathe in and out.

Tip: Imagine visiting other planets. What do you see? What do you feel?

Real-Life Scenarios

Life is full of adventures. There will be challenges. Things happen. Make good choices. These are some events you could face:

- You are planning a party. You have many things you need to do. How do you feel? Why is it important for you to be still for a moment? What could you meditate on?
- You have a lot on your mind. You have to get up early. But you can't get to sleep. There are too many thoughts running in your mind. What do you do? How can you calm your mind? What could you meditate on?
- You have a piano recital coming up. You don't feel ready. You keep making mistakes during practice. You are hard on yourself. How do you work on being more confident? What could you meditate on?

CHAPTER THREE
Use Music to Meditate

Music is very calming. There are many activities you can do with music. First, be mindful about your sense of hearing.

Use the sense of hearing as a way to be still. Close your eyes. Take a deep breath. Pretend your ears are very big. Pretend they're as big as your body. Your big ears can hear everything. Focus on sounds in the room. Spend a few minutes on each sound. Be still with each sound. Next, focus on sounds in the distance. Spend a few minutes on each sound. See how far you can go. Last, focus on the sound of your own breath.

Tip: Make a playlist. Include songs that bring up good memories.

Use music to spark creativity. Play **instrumental** music. Instrumental means music without singing. Listen carefully. Imagine the story the music is telling. Or do art while you listen.

Use music to develop a sense of hearing. Play instrumental music. Choose an instrument. Examples are piano, violin, and oboe. Listen only for that instrument. Follow that instrument throughout the music. Choose a different instrument to focus on. Listen to the music again.

Learn to play an instrument. Be mindful of how playing affects our body. Be mindful of how our body's movements affect the music. Practicing an instrument is like meditation. It requires focus. Respect your instrument. Be mindful of its power to make music.

Tip: Wear headphones. Block out noise with music. Focus on the music and nothing else.

CHAPTER FOUR
Chant Your Worries Away

Chants and **mantras** are good tools for meditation. Chants are repeated notes. Mantras are inspirational sayings. The idea is to repeat calming words while breathing. Sometimes, it's hard to slow down your thoughts. It's hard to be still. Say a mantra or chant. Repeat this process. This will help narrow your focus.

The most popular chant is "Om." Close eyes. Breathe in through nose. Breathe out. Chant "Om." Say it slowly. Say it loudly at first. Then, get softer. Breathe out. Repeat several times. Try to make the "om" sound last longer. Try to make it softer and softer. Close your mouth. Repeat the chant in your mind only.

Tip: Chant in a group. This can help you feel more connected.

Use mantras to focus on self-love. Sit still. Close your eyes. Recall a time when you felt deeply loved. Place a hand over your heart. Hold on to those warm feelings. Feel it deeply. Say to yourself, "May I be happy. May I be safe. May I be at peace." Repeat this. Imagine the warmth spreading from your heart to your whole body.

Use mantras to help heal fights. Sit still. Close your eyes. Think of the person you're fighting with. Become that person. See things from that person's perspective. Try to understand the other person. Send feelings of warmth. Say, "May you be happy. May you be safe. May you be at peace." Repeat this. Imagine this warm feeling spreading to that person.

Tip: Pick an important saying. Say it every morning when you get up. Say it every evening when you go to bed.

Science Connection

Meditation increases attention. It helps people focus more. It helps people be more mindful. It fights against habituation. Habituation is when we do things without thinking about it. It's when we stop paying attention to old information. It's when we tune out things. Habituation can be good. It allows us to focus on new information only. Our brain prioritizes important things. But it can also be bad. We stop noticing and responding. We become less mindful. Habituation is found in all types of animals. It's found in 1 type of plant. Habituation can be dangerous for wild animals. Animals need to survive. They need to protect themselves. They need to respond quickly. They need to be aware of predators. Predators are hunters. If animals get used to sounds, they won't be as alert. They won't be able to defend themselves. Being mindful makes us stronger. It makes us more aware.

Chapter Five
See with Your Eyes

Focus on the sense of sight. Seeing means being aware of your **surroundings**. Surroundings are things around us. This includes buildings, nature, and people. Mindful seeing makes us more alert.

Try "**Gazing** Meditation." Gaze means to stare with purpose.

- Make the room dark. Light a candle. (Be careful!)
- Sit 2 to 3 feet (61 to 91 centimeters) away from the candle.
- Gaze at the flame. Watch the flame move. Don't move your eyes. Do this for 2 minutes.
- Close your eyes. Picture the candle in your mind. Play with that picture. Try to move the candle in your mind. Imagine changing the color of the candle. Imagine changing the shape.

Tip: Work on developing all 5 senses. For smell, use essential oils. Essential oils come from plants.

Try "Board Drawing":

- Pick a favorite animal.
- Close your eyes.
- Pretend there's a board in front of your eyes.
- Draw your animal on the board. Draw it slowly. Draw a line at a time. Focus on each line.
- Open your eyes. Draw the animal from your imagination on paper.

Try "Mind Picture":

- Pick a favorite object. It could be a toy. It could be a picture. It could be a book cover.
- See all the details. Focus on 1 detail at a time.
- Close your eyes. Recall the object in your mind.
- Open your eyes. Take a look at the object.
- Close your eyes. Add more details to the picture in your mind.
- Repeat.

Tip: Focus on taste and touch. Get fruit. Touch it. Eat it slowly.

Fun Fact

There were once 33,061 people who meditated together. They logged in online. They meditated for 30 minutes. This happened on August 8, 2014. They set the world record for the largest online meditation in history. Participants came from all around the world. Over 100 countries were represented. Over 140,000 people were there. But only 33,061 counted for the world record. This event was led by Dr. Deepak Chopra. Chopra is an Indian American. He's a famous spiritual leader. He's an author and speaker. He said, "Peace can only be created by those who are peaceful . . . We wanted to explore what would happen if thousands of people around the world came together to be still in a meditation practice for peace. It was an incredible experience for everyone that participated."

Chapter Six
Have Fun with Beads

A **mala** is a string of beads. It's used for meditation. It has 108 beads.

Make your own mala bracelet. Get a long string. Add each bead slowly. Tie a knot on top of each bead. Be mindful about it. Breathe in and out as you add beads. Join the ends. Add a special bead or charm. This is called the **guru** bead. Guru means expert. Then, add a **tassel**. Tassels are dangling ornaments of loose threads.

You can use the beads in different ways. You can use them to count your breaths. Imagine each bead as a breath. Breathe in and out. Do this as you move your fingers from one bead to another. Roll the beads through your fingers. Pay attention to the beads. Focus on how the beads feel.

Tip: Grab hold of the beads whenever you're feeling anxious.

You can also use the beads to meditate:

- Hold the beads in your hands. Start with the bead to the right of the guru bead.
- Turn each bead with your fingers. Use your thumbs to turn the beads.
- Breathe in and out at each bead.
- Say a mantra at each bead. An example is to say something you're thankful for. Another example is to say, "I am ..." Say **positive** things. Positive means nice and kind.
- Slowly move to the next bead.
- Stop when you get to guru bead. This is the signal to be still. It's time to reflect.

Tip: Practice mantras with beads.

Spotlight Biography

Oprah Winfrey was born in 1954. She is a media superstar. She's an actress. She's a talk show host. She has her own TV network. She's the richest African American woman of the 21st century. She is North America's first black multibillionaire. She does a lot of community service. She gives away a lot of money. She strongly believes in meditation. She said meditation changed her life for the better. She promoted being still. She said, "The voice that truly matters is the silent voice of awareness, consciousness, aliveness . . . My advice is to start small. When you're in the shower or tub, simply be with the water." She makes meditation a habit. She works on being still for a period of time. She wants to connect with her real self. She meditates for 20 minutes in the morning. She also meditates for 20 minutes at night.

HOST YOUR OWN MINDFULNESS EVENT!

Feeling overwhelmed? Is your mind jumbled? Do you have too much to do? This might be the best time to host your own mindfulness event! Help yourself and others relax. Get in touch with yourself. Host a "Be Still" Party!

STEP ONE: Figure out where you can host your party. Consider being outside. Nature and fresh air are great for group meditations.

STEP TWO: Make invitations—and get creative! Ask a friend to help you. Send out the invitations.

STEP THREE: Gather supplies where needed. Lead the group meditations.

Take a Deep Breath!

Read this out loud in a calm and soft voice:

- Take a deep breath. Count to 3 while you breathe. Pause for 3 seconds. Breathe out for 3 seconds. Pause for 3 seconds. Start again.
- Breathe from your nose.
- Breathe from your mouth.
- Breathe from your throat.
- Breathe from your chest.

Be a Mountain!

Read this out loud in a calm and soft voice

- Close your eyes. Feel your whole body. Feel the position of your body. Feel the shape of your body. Feel how your body takes up space. Feel the weight of your body.
- Pretend your body is a mountain. Feel solid and firm on the ground.
- Focus on breathing out. Feel your body becoming more like a mountain.
- Think about your feelings. Think about topics. Do this for as long as you can.
- Breathe in. Feel your body getting back to normal.

Take a Walk!

- Take a walk with your friends.
- Get a metronome. Metronomes are devices that count beats. Set the metronome to a fast beat. You can also find a song with a fast beat.
- Everyone should follow the beat with their steps. (Every beat is 1 step.)
- Slow down the metronome. Or find a song with a slow beat. Slow down with the song. If you're the leader, ask everyone to think about what your body needs to do to slow down.
- Continue to slow down. Walk slower than the beat.
- Stop the metronome or song you're listening to.
- Use the beat of your breaths instead.

GLOSSARY

chants (CHANTS) repeated notes

gazing (GAYZ-ing) staring with purpose

guru (GOO-roo) expert

instrumental (in-struh-MEN-tuhl) music without any singing

mala (MAH-lah) string of 108 beads used for meditation

mantras (MAHN-truhz) sayings that inspire

meditation (med-ih-TAY-shuhn) a focused form of deep thinking for a period of time that leads to a calm state of mind

mindful (MINDE-ful) focusing one's awareness on the present moment to center the mind, body, and soul

positive (PAH-zih-tiv) thoughts and feelings that evoke happiness

surroundings (suh-ROUN-dingz) things around us like buildings, nature, and people

tassel (TAS-uhl) dangling ornament of loose threads

vibrations (vye-BRAY-shuhnz) sound waves

yoga (YOH-guh) the practice of quieting the mind by combining breathing techniques, exercise, and meditation

INDEX

About the Author

Dr. Virginia Loh-Hagan is an author, university professor, and former classroom teacher. Her meditation is playing piano. She lives in San Diego with her very tall husband and very naughty dogs.